The Magical Business Method

Define Your Stardust, Attract Your Tribe, Make Lots of Money

Tamara Arnold

Difference Press

McLean, Virginia, USA

Copyright © Tamara Arnold, 2018

Difference Press is a trademark of Becoming Journey, LLC

Published 2018

ISBN: 978-1-68309-224-7

DISCLAIMER

Cover Design: Jennifer Stimson

Editor: Maggie McReynolds

Author's photo courtesy of Sarah Bissell Photography

Advance Praise

"*The Magical Business Method* is an energetic blueprint for navigating the black-and-white world of business. Instead of relying on definitive business models, *The Magical Business Method* relies on beliefs, feelings, emotions, and the body's energy system of chakras. I loved how the book takes you through each chakra, what they mean, and how to integrate them into having a successful business. Tamara explains the Law of Attraction, and how to attract clients and work from home, which is brilliant. This is a great book for achieving success through your energy systems and beliefs. It's a must read for anyone who would like to be successful in their own business using energy work and Tamara's guidance."

JOANNE KING, AUTHOR – *TOO GOOD TO GO, TOO BAD TO STAY*

"I just finished reading *The Magical Business Method* by Tamara Arnold. I loved it. Tamara takes you through a wonderful explanation of the chakras - your body's energy centers – and strategies for clearing them in yourself and by doing so, infusing light and magic into your business. These strategies can also help in so many other areas of your life as well. Her mindfulness approach, her vulnerability, and her down-to-earth nature make this a wonderful tool for entrepreneurs and are the reasons why Tamara is an amazing coach and mentor. When I was a student in the Chakra Business Academy, Tamara was able to tap into my stardust (as she calls it) and leapfrog me to a place where I could finally get crystal clear on my soul's purpose. Her energy truly is engaging and magical. I would recommend the book and the Chakra Business Academy to anyone feeling stuck in their entrepreneurial journey."

TONI CARBONE, LIFE COACH - *FROM YOUR SOUL COACHING*

Dedication

I would like to dedicate this book to my husband,
Jeff Arnold, who stood beside me as I went from in debt
to best-selling author in five years. It's been a wild ride,
sometimes without a clear path. But no matter what life
threw at us, he was my rock, my support, and my love.
When I started to hear Angels, and then to read chakras,
he didn't even blink an eye. This kind of love is sacred.

Table of Contents

Introduction

I decree that we will mess everything up. And that is amazing. For years we have been told to keep everything together. Keep the house and kids tidy. Work. Smile. Do what we are expected. Stay within the comfort zone of those around us. Don't rock the boat. If your kids are driving you crazy, don't tell anyone. If you and your husband aren't getting along, seal your lips. It's no wonder that energetically, we begin to close ourselves off to sensing and hearing the incredible greatness around us. No human being can uphold the expectations of running that many things successfully without crashing. Computers crash. Women do, too. I want to break the status quo with this book. I want to give you permission to live a life of your choosing. One where you can work from home, be present with your kids on a level that feels good for both of you, and most importantly, where you don't have to do a darn thing for anyone else if you don't feel like it.

What if you could make your own rules, mess everything up, and still keep the kids and plants alive? OK, maybe not the plants. That's unrealistic. At least to me. But seriously.

Within you is the capacity to make a difference in the world. There is a catch, though. Perfection can't come along for the ride. Neither can fear, and for sure other people's beliefs need to stay home. If you are willing to energetically let go of these things, magic is going to happen.

Can you imagine what life would be like without the thought that life was hard? Who decided that, anyway! It took me until I was 38 before I realized that was a load of hokey. Hopefully, reading this book will help you see that that is a myth. Unreal. Made up to keep us small.

There are so many people living the same day over and over again. Wake up. Make breakfast and get the kids ready. Go to work. Come home, put the kids to bed, watch Netflix. Repeat. That is what everyone else is doing. Is that not normal? NO! There is an energetic world out there where you can create a life that lights you up. That releases you from the droning of monotony.

If you are reading this and think I'm crazy, this book is probably not for you. This book is not for the mom who is happy striving to achieve the perfect model of being a mother, woman, and businesswoman. In my world, perfection doesn't exist. Life is made for mistakes and celebrations. Declaring your truth and rocking the boat. Life is short. Tomorrow is not guaranteed. Leave the house and the kids messy.

This book is for the mom who is ready to take control of her time and her hours. The mom who wants to make her own magic, doing what she loves in her own house, where her kids are. The mom who is done being a cookie-cutter model of what everyone tells her to be. A rebel with a dream of making an impact on the world. A difference maker.

If this is you, let me introduce myself.

I'm a dreamer. The most social loner you will ever meet.

I live in books and believe in fairy tales. I tried for years to uphold the image of a perfect mom, even when my life was falling apart around me. It was insane.

When I finally let go of being someone I was not, for someone who didn't matter, the Universe sighed and gave me my gift: the gift to read energy and help other moms create a business that energetically lights them up from home. This way they can be home with their kids, live by their own rules, and make their own money. Lots of money. All the money they want. Because why not.

CHAPTER ONE

Lost My Job

For most of my life, I tried to keep one vital piece of my life secret. I sucked as a parent. Being the rebel-rule-breaker that I am, I got pregnant at 19 and started my job as a mother at 20. I didn't feel loved in so many areas of my life, so I decided my best opportunity was to create my own person to love. This plan seemed highly likely to succeed in my mind, but was way more difficult than I anticipated.

Being a parent is a full-time job. No holidays. Pay sucks. But once you sign the contract, you are locked in for the long haul. Good days, best days, and terrible days come with the territory. The funny thing is, most people only talk about the good and the best days. There aren't a lot of people running around saying how much their parenting day sucked. As in smeared-the-poop-on –the-wall, pulled-the-plant-over, cut-their-hair-off, and cried-all-day sucked.

Why do we do this? Sugar coat our lives like a candy for the world to see? Pretend everything is perfect and shiny and nothing bad is happening? I understand that walking around like a rain cloud is a drag for us and everyone else, but what happened to keeping it real?

I remember being little and complaining about not getting my way. My parents, like their parents before them, taught me the same "valuable" lesson: "Get used to it, life is hard." It was the beginning of a belief system that would last most of my life.

I accepted this as way of life. Everything needed to be hard. When I was a young mom, I worked two jobs to make ends meet. Nights at a bar, days at a hardware store. When I couldn't do that anymore, because three hours' sleep and a toddler don't mix, I worked as many hours as I could at a local restaurant. I remember feeling like I was missing something. There had to be a way to be home with Ethan and make money. I placed that thought in the back of my head and kept grinding.

Chances are you may be sensitive or an empath and that is why you picked up this book, so it will come as no surprise to you to hear that working in a restaurant was not the greatest thing for me. People were angry all the time. Food wasn't cooked properly. Everything took too long. It was too hot, too cold, not right. I can remember going home after work and feeling burdened, like I was wearing a weighted vest. Ethan would be so excited to see me, and I just felt bogged down. Heavy. Not the way I saw images of moms and sons in the magazines. Who were these people? What did they do for a living?

When I had had enough of the service industry, I signed up for an employment services program. I wanted to find a way to be happy with work and a better mom. Even in my 20s, I dreamed of a way to enjoy work and play. To have the perfect family. Days at the park with the kids, meeting the man of my dreams, living in a house with a wrap-around porch.

When the employment agency came up with "personal trainer" as a job that I would enjoy, it made perfect sense. As a sponge for other people's emotions, working in a place where everyone went to feel better seemed too good to be true. I could eat that up energetically! My problems were solved. I had thoughts of becoming the next famous television trainer, although I would have been happy with the local channel 10 station with a lunch-hour fitness class. Pumped up like a peacock, I told the ones I loved my plans. The response I got would become an energetic blueprint that I carried for years. "Good luck making a living with that" became a silent thought that swirled in my head.

It's so crazy that we become the thoughts we hear as kids, but when someone in our lives who we respect says something, we make it truth. Tuck it up in our DNA as being the only option. We carry it around, letting it guide our decisions and thoughts, until one day it doesn't fit anymore. It feels foreign and gross.

I was in a seminar when this happened. I had recently left training and was trying to figure out my next role. I'd spent the year working through how to have an online business that would help people all over the world. I'd taken programs and invested time and money, but I still didn't quite have the answer. It was so close I could taste it.

The man teaching was a wonderful Indian man, he oozed peace of mind. Just being in a room with him made me want to fulfill my potential and then some. In one of the sessions, he talked about how the world taught us how to make things hard, but in truth, it could be easy. He invited us to imagine a world where we taught our kids that anything was possible, and money was everywhere.

At this time, I had married the man of my dreams, and was sharing my life with him, my daughter from a previous relationship, my son (who I already mentioned), and a step-daughter and stepson. I had just quit my job, and Christmas was approaching. I raised my hand, shaking slightly, and asked the question burning in my chest. I asked, "So telling my kids that we have no money for Christmas this year, that I'm not working and not to expect much, was a bad idea?"

"Yes!" the man exclaimed. "Every day is Christmas. Tell your kids they can have anything they want when they want it."

I was still confused. "But won't they tell you they want everything and become spoiled?"

He smiled at me. "No," he said, "they will learn that life doesn't have to be hard, and that they can achieve anything."

I went home that day, piled the kids in to the living room and apologized for the way I had spoken about money and told them that I wanted them to see that life had limitless possibilities. I promised to help change the way they saw the world and to step fully into parenting and modeling the belief that every day was Christmas. Was I nervous they would go crazy? Yep! Do you want to know what actually happened? The previous script that we had no money and life was hard just kept playing.

I took my daughter shopping and she told me she didn't need the clothes she tried on. She calculated the cost of the four items in the dressing room, and they totalled 55 dollars. That was too much, she said. I cringed. What had I done? I had led her to believe this.

When my business started to take off, we took my daughter and stepdaughter out to our favourite restaurant. It is the most adorable Italian place – low ceilings, close tables, homemade food. They opened the menus, and my stepdaughter closed hers immediately. "We can't eat here," she said. When I asked why, she replied, "Because the meals are like 20 dollars each!"

My daughters were 11 when this happened. At 11, they already believed that life was hard and that money wasn't for us. I had a lot of work to do.

I grew up watching my mom balance her chequebooks. It was always clear that you kept a close eye on what went in and what went out. Bills got paid first, and if anything was left over, that is what you used. I am so grateful for that lesson. I always kept a firm hold on the thought that my bills got paid first. This came in handy when I moved out at 17. No matter how out of control my life got, the first thing I did was make sure that my utilities were paid. Then I went partying. But I also believed that money was hard to attain and that we never had enough. I still check my bank account every morning. Some habits are hard to break.

My dad grew up with parents who believed that you let your kids figure things out. So that was his lesson for us: Money didn't grow on trees. If you got yourself into financial trouble, it was your job to get yourself out. Knowing I didn't have a fallback plan allowed me to figure things out on my own, but it also left me feeling lost on how to handle money.

I always worked hard and made the money I needed, until the day I couldn't do it anymore. My son had behavioural issues: depression and Oppositional Defiance Disorder (ODD). After years of trying to work and take care of him, my life crumbled around me. His needs were too great. I needed to be home. I tried to step down to part-time at my job, but part-time wasn't part of their policy. It was time to go out on my own and figure things out.

I had no roadmap. No idea. And my life was tornado of appointments, calls from the school, and putting out fires at home. At this time, I was a single mom. My daughter was four and my son was 12. There was no manual on how to make money when your life was falling apart and you had to work from home. The only thing that I did know how to do was keep the door closed and pretend life was way better than it was.

The next three years until I met my husband were up and down. I struggled in my business, trying to balance being there for my kids with making enough to pay my bills. Because bills came first. I took on credit card debt to pay for groceries and gas, but always made my mortgage. I kept everything to myself and never let anyone know what was going on. Why do we do this? All I wanted was for everyone to think I had it all together. It's crazy.

When I met my husband, I was in debt, a half-ass businesswoman, and an incredible hider of my secrets. Recently, as I was driving (using Bluetooth, no worries), I thanked him for coming along on my journey. In five years, I have completely changed my financial situation, dealt with my money issues, and written a book about being a mom with a child with mental illness. I feel like I have become a different person.

He told me he didn't know why he was interested in me at first. I checked all the boxes of what not to date. I owed a lot of money, seemed like a party girl (at least, in my own backyard), and had a chaotic life. It didn't make sense to him. Then he said the words that melted my heart and made sense to me. He told me he fell in love with the woman he knew I would be. The one who was calling him on the phone and thanking him for the journey.

So how did I go from being a broke single mother to giving my husband the choice to retire, in five years? The first thing I had to do was let go of everything everyone else had ever taught me. I needed to become a clean slate, seeing the world in a way where there were endless possibilities, money was everywhere, and it could be easy. So many people in the world have figured out this secret already.

I just needed to tap into that energy. I needed to use the magical equation that has become the very basis for my life. I needed to believe that anything was possible. Trust that the Universe would bring it to me. And take the action steps to make magic happen.

What Now?

Quit your job. No seriously. If you hate it and it makes you completely unhappy, life is too short to simply exist. Dreading the day. Feeling miserable. Taking it out on the ones you love. It doesn't have to be this way. I am not saying to go right this second and fire off a letter of resignation. But I am suggesting that there is another way to make money and live life.

I was forced to leave my job because my life was falling apart around me. I had no fallback plan. I didn't even have a chance to look for something "in the meantime." Ethan needed me to be home, period. But once I hit the road to self-employment, I never looked back. Did I freak out sometimes and question if I was making the right decision? Oh, heck yeah! Especially in the beginning, when I didn't know what I was doing.

Going from set paycheques and structure can be an adjustment, especially when you jump off the cliff without a plan. Having an idea of what you want to be doing and how you are going to help people is kind of important.

Just kidding, it's super important! But that's all you need. You don't need a website and you don't need business cards. Neither of these things matter if you don't have any people to help.

Once upon a time, I needed to make money for a big payment I had coming up. I had invested the most I ever had in taking a program for myself, and the next pay date was looming. I called up my virtual assistant (VA) and went into a fast-talking pitch. I was going to need a ton of help and support to create material and a webinar. I was going to launch my own program, *Awaken to Life*, in three weeks. I totally believed that with no list, no connection to anyone, and no idea what I was doing, somehow magically people would find this program I was launching helpful, even though it didn't solve anyone's problems. Who doesn't want to *Awaken to Life*? It's what you are sitting here thinking about right now as you read this. Should I make chicken for dinner tonight, or do I want *to Awaken to Life*?

It was a disaster. No one showed up to my webinar except some friends. (Thank you for your support, by the way.) I took out Facebook ads that didn't connect to anyone, so no one signed up. I spent $1100 to help no one. Not a single soul. This could have been the moment I gave up. But the opposite happened.

I realized I was hiding. It was so much easier to put up a bunch of pretty pictures and hope that people would find me than it was to reach out and try to connect with them. The phone scared me. But it finally clicked one day. If you don't talk to people, how do you know if you are supposed to help them? If you need people to work with to make money, wouldn't the first thing you look for be people?

The quest to get people on the phone began. I broke down all my fears, all my walls, and bared my naked soul out in to the world for all to see. And guess what happened next? One, people are starving to connect and share in your journey. So being emotionally naked was a good thing. Two, I started to talk to people. I listened for a problem they had, and I offered to solve it with them. Then, one day, it happened. I got a "yes"! I can still remember where I was sitting when I had my first "yes." I hung up the phone and just let the moment sink in. That day changed my life.

Have you ever created a story for something before you've done it? Imagined an outcome happening (or ten)? I used to have so many stories of what people would think about me, or say about me if I showed as who I really was. The neighbours would gossip. My family would disown me. People would think I was crazy. But who I am, a unicorn-riding, New-Kids-on-the-Block-loving, enchanted fairy is completely normal. And for those who don't understand that, I can't be friends with them anyway!

Getting rid of the stories we tell ourselves is super important in the journey of finding who we are and what we want out of life. Do you feel you are the only one who can do things? Do you need to make sure things are perfect before you begin? Have you started things and not completed them because you don't think people would want them? This is the stuff that doesn't help you or the people who need you.

When people sign up to work with me, it's because they are ready to get rid of the garbage that isn't serving them to bring in the things that are. My clients go from having no idea how to run a business from home to making upwards of $10,000 a month. It isn't rocket science. There are no fancy gimmicks. It's about finding who you are meant to help, getting them on the phone, and then helping them. Boom. Mic drop. You can go off and make millions of dollars now. But in truth. You actually can.

My client Alison went from frustrated and angry with herself and her business to loving what she did in only a few weeks with me. She was my favourite call I have ever had. When I asked her why she had reached out to talk to me, her exact answer was, "Your post pissed me off." How intriguing! I asked her why my post pissed her off and she clipped out, "I'm pissed that you have figured it out and I haven't. Why are you making money and I'm not?!" I was utterly fascinated with this response.

Our conversation was like locking horns, and in the end, I simply stated, "Clearly you have everything figured out, unless you are just looking for someone to hold you accountable? In which case, if you are, I can do that." She agreed that was what she wanted, and a beautiful relationship was born. Within a month, she was pulling in thousands of dollars in her business. She dumped everything that had been part of the story of why she couldn't have what I had, and owned the story that she could.

Alison showed up, for herself and her tribe, and magic happened. It's still happening. Recently she declared she is going to Mexico for six months to flush out who she is, and by sharing her journey on social media, she is bringing us with her. She is inviting us along by sharing her story. All while working and making a difference in the world.

Then there was Kristie. Kristie was working two jobs and wasn't getting where she wanted very quickly. Her son was struggling with some mental health issues, and she wanted to be home with him more. When she saw the success I was having, she wanted to figure it out. What I love about Kristie is she is one of the biggest skeptics that I know and she questions everything. How could she possibly go from working for others to working from home and making more money than she currently did? It didn't make sense. I love when people are open to learning, even when they can't fathom the outcome.

There was some serious resistance in the beginning, which I think is amazing! If you aren't feeling uncomfortable, there can't be major shifts happening. Within a month of working together, she had brought in more than twice what she had paid to work with me. How amazing is that? That's what I want for you.

The thing is, I am no different than you. I don't have special sauce, or horseshoes up my butt. I am not a witch. OK, maybe I am, but I am a good witch. Like Glinda. I am simply an energy reader who decided that life was full of possibilities and that success had to be easier than the *fear* of success. Easy became my motto, and I started a new conversation with myself. One that included never saying "I'm tired," "I'm hungry," "I'm bored," or any other "I am" statements that called crap to me.

I made a new script for myself, one that was already inside me. I listened to hear the magic and answered its calling. This is not a secret. I am not holding anything back from you. Everything I did is in these pages. You will be able to have it all too. It all begins with opening your mind. And then opening your heart.

CHAPTER THREE

Define Your Stardust

Here's where all the magical stuff starts to happen. What if I told you that you were born from the stars and that when you were placed here on Earth, embedded in your heart was a speck of stardust? This speck of stardust contains your mission. Your purpose. It is there for you to find. It is there so you can serve the world with your light.

When we are born into the bodies we have now, there is a reason we pick the life we lead. It could be for the lessons we need to learn, the people we need to meet, or the experience we need to have. As we peer down from the stars, we pick our parents, and our paths, long before we are born.

Have you ever thought, "There has to be a reason I've gone through this?" The answer is yes. You absolutely needed to go through what you have. Walk your very path. What you have lived through or accomplished allows you to reach back and serve the person walking behind you. For every step forward you take, there is someone a step behind who needs your help.

When I was in victim mode, my thoughts were all about why things were happening to me. How could someone be given so much sadness and hurt? Watching my mom suffer from depression, then going through so many hardships with my son. Clearly the world had it out for me. There was nowhere I could run, nowhere I could hide. Mental illness always found me.

I lived in fear for years. Afraid to talk about my story. Afraid to piss off my family. It was an awful place to be. I lived in silence. If you know me, silence is not my thing. Eventually the dam broke.

I believe our lives are unfolding to help bring us to our starlight. All we have to do is listen. When I stopped running from mental illness, that's when I heard mine. That's when I realized that everything that happened throughout my life was all guiding me to help serve the mom behind me. When I wrote *My Kid Is Driving Me Crazy: A Mom's Survival Guide for Living with a Child with Mental Illness,* I was petrified. I even tried to write a different book. The mission of standing up to tell my story, to help other moms going through what I went through, scared the snot out of me. If I didn't have an Angel sitting on my shoulder the whole time, I don't know if I could have done it. Thank you, Angel.

Listening to your stardust isn't always comfortable. It requires courage and bravery. Going to a place where you see the world as happening for you instead of to you means you leave fear at the door. The thoughts of what others are thinking don't matter anymore. You no longer need the approval of family and friends, because they aren't the ones you are here to help. You stop trying to make the people who will never be happy with your decisions happy. You find the people who your story will help, and you go all in.

When I was given an Angelic download to start doing chakra readings, without even studying them, I accepted the gift and the mission. Why not. Why would I receive such an awesome message from Source if it wasn't to serve? Was I scared? You bet. Was I determined to do as many as I could? 100 percent. Did I shake like a leaf when I started talking to strangers about what was going on in their energy systems? Big time. But I knew this was exactly where I needed to be. I knew this was my stardust speaking, so I listened. Within each chakra is the key to releasing what isn't serving you, to call in what is.

What makes it so hard to listen to your stardust? Chances are that somewhere along the way, you got side-tracked. You began living your life for someone else, like I did with my son, and not for you anymore. This happened to me for 17 years, and even when I started to hear my guidance, it would take another year for me to let go of my fear of judgement. Letting go of what your family, friends, and neighbors think is a hard pattern to break. Seeking the approval of those we love is anchored deep in our DNA. But what if no matter how hard you try, you will never get that approval? How many years do you keep trying? What if you took all that energy and used it to step into your light instead? What if it was possible to surround yourself with a new tribe, one that matched your vibration and changed how you looked at the world?

Once you let go of needing to be someone you are not, that's when the fun begins. You are ready to shine your light. Now you get to stand up in front of everyone you know and declare your purpose. Easy peasy, right? Cue the panic! Stardust requires strength and courage. It requires you to stand fully in your power, confidently sharing your mission with the world. Living each moment as it happens, without holding on too tight.

That means you need to tune out all the stories that others have given you, that time when Uncle Jimmy said you were nothing but a silly little girl, or the years when your parents never wanted to hear what you had to say. These are not your truths, and believing them stops you from stepping into your light. You need to be ready to create a new belief about yourself. One that says your words matter and you are worthy of greatness. When you can hold those thoughts in your mind, you will be ready to shine.

Now you need to receive. Oh yeah, baby! Let all the good stuff flow in. Fill your days with compliments, love, affection, kind words, clients, and money. You need to fill your heart with love in every form, so it can sing and dance with your stardust. When your stardust is bursting with love, it means you can shine it out like a care bear stare over everything and everyone you meet. It's a big love fest, in the most G-rated way. Love flows in, love flows out.

You can't keep it contained anymore. You want to scream from the rooftops that you are in bliss. Serving the person you are here to serve, full of light. How will you get your message out? Do you want to make videos or write poems? Words are powerful. Figuring out if your voice or your written word is your super power will catapult your mission into homes all over the world. Buckle up, when you are ready to speak, amazing things happen. People start listening, and they pick up what you are putting out.

Can you trust that all this can happen? Can you go into the unknown knowing that everything is going to be ok? That there are no wrong directions, only movement toward your dreams? This is the beautiful key to unlocking magic. When you trust that the Universe is supporting you, even when you fail, you succeed. Everything is a lesson meant to learn from. You love every experience that happens and thank the stars you are living your dreams.

At this point, you are like an energetic firecracker of awesome. You know your stardust, you are living your truth. It's time to order from the Universal drive-through of life. You can call in clients, money, experiences, trips. The world is your oyster, and all you see are pearls. Here you realize that you can choose to call in only good things. There is no need to live in misery, guilt, or shame. You can have a beautiful life, with beautiful things. You are full on magic. Sparkling everywhere.

Your story holds your stardust, and when you listen to your heart, you can hear it. This is the first step in defining what you are on this Earth to do. Don't be afraid to ask your heart for yours. You can uncover your light and shine it in the world. If there is anything blocking you, know that that is what the rest of this book is for. The next seven chapters go through each chakra and guide you to clear out what isn't serving you in order to bring in what is. Follow along, and clear your energy in all areas of your life. Start by writing out some notes about your life. In your notes you will see why you have lived the life you have. That you have gone through what you have for a reason. When you find that, you have found your stardust.

CHAPTER FOUR

Your Tribe Vibe

ROOT CHAKRA

Resistance*:*

Distraction

Energy*:*

House and home

Tribe vibe or people you are here to serve

Characteristics*:*

Acceptance

Belonging

Connection

Inclusion

Side Effects*:*

Seeking the approval of others

Fearing the judgment of others

People pleasing

No boundaries

Goal of clearing this chakra: To not give a crap what others think so you can be present to connect to your stardust and your tribe.

The root chakra is the basis of who we are. It is our desire to fit into a group/tribe/clan/posse, whatever you want to call it. It is the need to feel accepted by those around us. If you don't have a connection to your parents, didn't have any friends in high school, never fit in at work, or have trouble connecting to others, chances are, your root chakra isn't vibrating very high.

This totally effs up your ability to serve the people you were put on this earth to serve. You end up trying to fit into a tribe that was never meant for you in the first place. It's exhausting, and you never get anywhere.

Not that long ago, everything that could be going wrong in my root chakra was going wrong. I couldn't understand why my personal training business was sucking the big one. Nothing seemed to be working. I posted on Facebook, contacted people, was full of hope, but everything felt hard. Tamara's Training (original name I know!) was flopping.

When things were going well, I was working 13-hour days and was zombie mom. Everyone around me felt the repercussions. I would walk in from work, sit in my chair, and be asleep within minutes. There could be an epic Star Wars battle going on in my living room, but I would be sitting there, mouth opening, drooling away.

So why did everything seem so hard? I was rocking a seriously fractured root chakra. I exhibited every side effect listed above, and was so disconnected from being present in myself that I was oblivious.

Seeking the approval of others

Oh, man, did this one live strong in me. It began early too. I can still remember being told young that I was an accident. The result of a stormy night in January 1977. It's amazing what being told you weren't planned can do to you from an early age. It can become the foundation of the thought, "I was never wanted."

The truth is I spent most of my life waiting to hear the words, "I'm proud of you" from my father. I mean YEARS! It was very clear early on that my lack of continuing education in the traditional school system did not make him happy. It felt more like he was embarrassed of it. There would be comments made, that he would be the only one in his life who had made this good decision.

When I knew my life was meant to serve and I found personal training, I felt light fill me in a way I had not felt before. I was so excited for myself, for the people I would help, and for finding a job that felt so right. When I excitedly told him that this was what I was going to do, I received, "Good luck making a living out of that." I was crushed.

It felt like nothing I ever did was good enough, so I tried harder. There had to be something I could create, make of myself, or do that would have him shouting from the rooftops that I was his daughter, and he had never been prouder in his life. It wasn't until last year that I realized I wasn't meant to get his approval. That I can be in the presence of great love with him, but my dad was never meant to be a part of my movement. My tribe.

When I started my intuitive life coaching business last year, I finally surrendered my need for his approval. I stopped telling him what I was doing, because he didn't understand and had little nice to say about it. Instead, I surrounded myself with the people who were lighting up my life, raising my vibration. I could show up fully for those who were part of my clan, free of needing confirmation that what I was doing was good. It felt like a huge weight had been lifted off me.

I remember when I started working with Jessica. She felt as though she was suffocating in her life. When I read her energy, her root chakra was completely turned off. She had no sense of who she was anymore. The loneliness and sadness she felt were overwhelming her.

We started working together to find out where the basis of these thoughts had come from. She never felt like she fit in with her family, her brothers called her names, like stupid and an idiot. It didn't help that she didn't fit in in school, either, so when she found a friend, she became what she felt that friend wanted her to be.

Her entire life had been built on trying to fit in with people who didn't make her feel good and took advantage of her, and she felt like crap because of it. We started clearing her root chakra energy and revelation after revelation happened. How long she had tried to get her family to accept her, and how many friends had walked over her, simply because she wanted their approval.

Serious magic happens when you see someone wake up and realize that the energy they had been putting toward trying to fit in with the wrong group could be changed to create space to serve the right group.

Jessica has an incredible mission to help women whose partners suffer from mental illness work through the challenging times so they can have beautiful, loving marriages. She is an energy worker and incredible mother. When we started to bring her to a space of being around people who shared her thoughts, feelings, and vibrations, there was a glow that erupted from her. She stepped into the space of connecting with the exact people she was meant to be surrounded by. The need to make her family happy and her friends happy disappeared. She showed up for those who needed her. Her business took off.

Fearing the judgments of others

Growing up around mental illness meant I had to watch what I said. I did not want to be the reason someone close to me fell into sadness. Then I became a mother of a child who suffered from mental illness, and my life turned dark for almost a decade.

I felt like everything was my fault. I couldn't help my family. I was a terrible daughter because I couldn't make my mom happy, and I was a terrible mom because I couldn't make my son better.

I hid all of this for a long time. There was so much fear that if I talked about what was happening, people would think I sucked. Sucked at being a daughter, and sucked at being a mother. I stopped telling people what was going on, especially when things with my son got bad, because they would clearly blame me. And when he chose to live on the streets over seeking help to come home, you better believe I disappeared into my hole and stopped talking to people completely.

What could I say that wouldn't be judged? I was paralyzed by what was happening, petrified that if anyone found out, they would disown me and spread hateful messages everywhere. I made assumptions of how people would react before even trying. I created an illusion of fear around myself. Wrapped up like a sushi roll on my couch.

The truth is, people are way more supportive than you think they are when you open up about the challenges you are facing. We live in world where we feel alone because everyone thinks they will be judged, so they don't share. You can imagine my surprise when I shared what had been happening in my life and realized that I had actually been through all this to turn around and help the person behind me.

This is the place where most of my clients struggle: with the realization that sharing is caring and nothing bad will happen. My favourite story is about my client Irene. She wrote the most beautiful Facebook post about how her father had left her at a very early age. He had dropped her and her mother off at a new house in a new town and said he would be right back. They never saw him again.

She had refused to post it because she felt everyone would judge her for what had happened. We spent 45 minutes talking while she freaked out and told me that everyone would be talking about it. Her neighbours would judge her, her friends would scorn her, and it would become the local gossip at all the coffee shops. After full-on freak out mode, she pressed post on Facebook, completely overwhelmed by fear of what others would think.

Do you know what happened? NOTHING. She received beautiful messages of love and support. The floor did not open, she was not swallowed whole, and no one in her neighbourhood or local coffee shops said a word. She opened the door for others to feel accepted. She created a space where they felt safe talking to her.

Her goal, when she started working with me, was to leave her office space so she could be home with her twin boys. When she released her fear of what others would think or say, she quickly created an online coaching business that allowed her to work from home. She stepped out of fear and into love.

People pleasing

My people pleasing is also known as codependency. I want to save those who do not want to be saved. This included my family, friends, and in the beginning, my clients. I just want to help so much it hurts sometimes.

The problem with people pleasing is you start to exist outside of your body. You worry about what your dad needs, your children, your partner, the person across the street, the mailman, or anyone else but yourself.

You create a world where you live outside your body instead of inside it. Like having an out-of-body experience, except it never goes away. When my son and I stopped talking a couple years ago, I remember walking into my living room and feeling so lost. I had lived solely for him for so long, I didn't know who I was anymore. It was the weirdest thing. There was nothing but emptiness inside me. It felt like a spark had gone out.

Giving yourself up to please the people around you forces you to completely forget about your needs. It creates a space where you are afraid to be yourself. Before you make a decision or speak in public, you wonder if the other person will like it. You become a pushover, giving up what you want so the other person is happy. You go to where they want to go for dinner, or to the movie they want to see instead of the one you have been dying to see since the trailer came out. So long as they are happy, you are happy.

My client Michelle was a huge people pleaser before we started working together. It was our biggest challenge, in fact. She was great at home, completely herself, but the minute she went to do anything for her business or step out of her house, boom, she morphed into the person who did what others wanted.

It took some time, but we got her to a place where she was authentic to her. She spoke with a clear voice in her business and with others, and it was incredible. Her business became exactly what she wanted it be, working with the exact people she was meant to help. By coming fully back into her body, she was able to stop spending her time trying to please others, and could create a business that she loved instead.

No boundaries

Come on, you know this has been you before. You say "yes" when you really want to say "no." You feel bad because the person you are going to help has no one else who can help them, or you think you will let them down. So you wake up on the weekend, take your grandma to the store, drive your kids to their friends, help Susie prep for her dinner party, and clean up after. You look back on the day, and you have done nothing for yourself.

And why would you? That would be selfish. Can you imagine spending time meditating, journaling, or going for a run? How could you do these things, when others need you?

That is exactly how my client Amanda felt when we started working together. She felt guilty about doing anything that took her away from the needs of those around her. It felt alien to give herself permission to do the things that made her feel good.

Here's the thing. Boundaries are key in creating a business that you love. It's up there as one of the top most important things you can do. In truth, boundaries are just as important in your personal life as well, but in business, holy moly, they are a must.

Take, for instance, writing this book. If I didn't create a strong boundary that I would not be accepting invitations to dinner parties, events, or helping people until it was done, I wouldn't be able to help the people reading this book. Does it piss some people off? Yep! Is it worth it? Yep!

Giving up the need to make people who don't care happy is completely freeing! Being willing to walk away from the negative people so you can surround yourself with positive people is the best. Your vibration raises, you feel like you are making a difference in the world, and you get to help others. It's the greatest healthy drug in the world.

Your root chakra being clear feels like a beam of light out into the Universe, calling all the magical people into your life. You stop worrying about what others are thinking, and do what feels good for you. You make different decisions. You realize that instead of trying to fit into a tribe/clan that was never meant for you, you get to become the leader and create your own. You can choose to surround yourself only with the people who make you feel good all the time!

When this happens, the energy at home changes. Your house is the space where you can be fully present for you. If you have strong boundaries, you stop trying to please others and seek approval before you move forward. You don't care what others are thinking. You, my friend, are in the perfect space to create a business.

After doing so many chakra readings, I've found a trend in how resistance affects each chakra. Be aware of how the root chakra resistance affects your house and home. It makes you unable to stay focused on the task at hand. You sit down to do something, and all of the sudden, the dishes need doing or laundry needs folding or you have to organize the kid's rooms. I call this Distraction Debbie, and she comes out when you are trying to move yourself forward in your life or business, and you just can't seem to focus.

Knowledge is power, so knowing that distraction is a form of moving forward in your business, you can make shifts to change it. I completely had to clean my entire office before starting to write my book. It was the most beautiful distraction, and I remained present for it. My goal is to honour my resistance, because I know that on the other side of it is greatness. I totally talk to my resistance as well, which may seem weird, but works for me. I told Distraction Debbie, that I was glad she came to make my office so beautiful, but when I was ready to write, she needed to stop harassing me. I did not need to clean anything else to begin. We agreed, and here I am. Being fully present to connect with the people I am here to serve.

CHAPTER FIVE

Sex and Money

SACRAL CHAKRA

Resistance*:*
Hiding
Energy*:*
Feminine
Sexual
Sensual
Characteristics*:*
Nurtured
Seen
Confident
Present
Side Effects*:*
Needing to be in control
Wanting to hide from the world
Not being present
Feeling sadness

Goal of getting this chakra cleared: Feeling bad ass in your body and oozing sexuality while bringing in the big bucks.

The sacral chakra is pure magic. When you can get this chakra thrumming, your business is going to be bringing in all the good coinage. A fully vibrating sacral has you showing up for everything in your life, fully present, oozing sexuality, confident in all you are doing. This, with a little money mindset work, will send you into the world of delicious sexuality and money opportunities galore.

This does not mean you will be working the streets selling your body for sex. It does mean that how you feel about your body matters. Learning to love every inch of yourself is the radical key to making major changes in your life.

Up until last year, I lived a life of victimhood. Everything happened *to* me. I had a sordid past with men, never connecting, always trying to find love in all the wrong places. You could play Rihanna's *I Found Love in a Hopeless Place* as my theme song. It was bad.

Confidence was the opposite of how I felt. It was more like, desperate. You could even say needy. I wanted someone to save me from my life. Where was Richard Gere when I needed him? I didn't like the inside or the outside of myself, which reflected back the lack of success I had in my life.

Staying hidden was my forte. Don't get me wrong, I'm loud. You could hear me in a crowd. But when it came to being seen professionally, I would choose hiding in a back room over stepping into my light. I broke down in a panic attack at the mere thought of speaking to my managers... also police officers and border patrol people. They all scare me, too.

Needing to stay in control

Being strong all the time sucks. I came by it honestly, though, it was a form of praise from my family. "Tamara, you are the strong one." The glue that holds us all together. I loved feeling that important for many years in my life. I felt that sense of need and worth. The problem was that it was too much for me handle.

Becoming a mom at 20, keeping my family together, figuring out who I was. Easy. No problem. I could keep it all under control. That's what I told myself. But the truth was, I couldn't. What ended up happening is I started to withdraw. I drank. I wanted to feel numb because the pressure of looking after everyone was too much for me.

Did anyone see this side of me? Sometimes. But only when I cracked a little, or something became so big that I couldn't find a way to shove it deep into some part of myself. When I left my house to go out in public, the mask was on. Everything was OK, and I could handle it. I didn't need anyone's help.

When I was forced to deal with my emotions a couple years ago, that's when I went deep into my sacral. I chose to let the feelings of needing to appear strong and in control all the time go. I was ready to be seen as the soft, fluffy unicorn I really am.

My client Heather was the same way. Working on her sacral plexus was emotional and very challenging. She admitted she liked staying in control because it kept her safe, comfortable. If she let down the mask, she would have to deal with emotions she had bottled up for 17 years.

Working with Heather was amazing because she was open to going deep. She was ready to let go. This allowed her to realize that every time she was about to work through this, let her mask go, and step into the next version of herself, she'd go into a funk. She was so done with feeling safe and small. Once we got clear that the "funk" was HER resistance to growth, she proceeded to release the mask, and the same day had multiple people reach out to her to coach.

Even going into writing this chapter, I had to let go of my control. I had gotten myself into a real tizzy with having to show up every day, market, be the sole breadwinner, write a book, and I felt myself slipping down the slippery slope of needing the mask and to stay in constant control.

Usually when I am overwhelmed I can hear a strong masculine voice in my head saying, "Do you trust me?", and of course I did. But that voice wasn't there. Which made me feel even MORE alone. That's when I heard HER (the feminine energy of Goddess/Mother Mary) voice. A beautiful voice that said, "Lie back into my arms, I am here to support you. You are safe and nurtured."

It was in this moment that I truly felt the feminine energy of the sacral work through me. That we can trust her to support us when we need to lean on her.

When I released the control to her, I felt my energy come back, and I was able to step back into my body as me. Without the mask and fully present to serve. This energy allowed the next three people I talked to to feel that love and support, and they all chose to work with me.

Wanting to hide from the world

There are times in our lives when the last thing we want to do is go out. It could be that the man of your dreams tells you he's leaving. You may lose someone close to you. It may be that you have always been a hider, never one to go out. Hiding for me is a like a roller coaster ride. Sometimes I want to be out all the time, vibrant and happy. Other times, I want to stay in my pajamas for months and eat ice cream.

My life definitely had many ups and downs in the hiding department. Even when I was going out, it was usually to drink and forget. I can say with great confidence, that I was an A-grade hider. I was exceptional. I used my ability to make people laugh, and my lack of using a filter as my shield. I was once given the nickname TMIT – Too Much Information Tamara. It was easy to keep the chaos of my home life hidden when I talked about my periods.

When I got tired of feeling bad about myself, who I was, and what my life situation had become, I started to work on me. I began working out regularly with a friend, cut out the crap that made my body feel bad, and started journaling. I still wasn't going out, but I began to like myself more, and feel that I had something to contribute to the world.

I felt so good I even joined Match.com. As a hider, there is nowhere else you go to look for a man.

Having found a space within myself that I liked, and shining that warm glow of awesome out into the world, my husband had no choice. I was irresistible. It was almost love at first sight (I don't remember all the details of our first date ... darn tequila!). But the one thing that stood out about Jeff that I will never forget is that at the end of each date, he would say, "When can I see you again?"

Years later, this is how I feel about connecting with my tribe. I don't ever want them to feel like I will post a message to them, do a Facebook live, and then not call again for weeks. I want them to know that I am there for them, that I love spending time with them, and that they can always depend on me. I want all the hiders out there to know I see them and honour their amazingness.

It takes confidence in yourself to step out and be fully seen. To choose to stand completely in your body, fearlessly demanding life give you everything it has to offer. NO hiding, NO shame, NO fear. This means there needs to be a big conversation between you, your body, and your belief in what you do.

When I started working with Jackie, she was quite comfortable staying in her sweats while trying to launch her business. She wrote posts on Facebook, but found the only way she was getting clients was through referrals from the people she was already working with.

In our first call together, there was a major shift that happened. She realized that she was petrified of being seen, and that she had been hiding her story and what she had been through in order to keep herself from having success. She was choosing to keep herself from her power, hiding in her house so that she wouldn't need to actually get out and do anything.

She had gone through a terrible few years with illness, and the medications she'd had to take had caused weight gain. As a wellness coach, she had felt like a fraud, and she was embarrassed. Where she saw weakness, I saw a beautiful story of strength, courage, and the fight to live. What an incredible story to share with the world.

It didn't take long for her to come back into her body, own her strengths, share with her tribe, and show up in a way that people felt her. As you guessed, her business began to boom, because she got confident in her message, and used her story to bring the right people she could help to her.

That's the thing about being seen. When you aren't hiding, and instead you show up each day, confident, people will be drawn to you. They will want to pick up what you are putting out.

Not being present

We all know that person. They come out to functions, and parties, but you just don't understand who they are, or what they do. They kind of have a glazed look in their eyes, get distracted, and sometimes, they walk away while you are talking to them. It's as though they didn't even notice that you were in a conversation. You are left standing there, opened-mouthed, thinking, what just happened?

It's as though they can't focus or connect. Listening is clearly not their strong suit. Maybe they interrupt every sentence you begin. Or perhaps they get loud and need all the attention. These are side effects of not being able to slow down and stay fully connected.

When I was younger, I had the attention span of a gerbil. I could not stand still, sit still, or listen to any long stories. As you can tell, I was not the greatest student. I got sooooo bored. Teachers were the worst (although they really are the best). They talked and talked about all the things I didn't want to know about. It honestly felt like torture to me. I had good grades, but I hated sitting in one spot all day.

It took practice for me to stop interrupting people when we were talking. I can be a highly excitable person, and when I have something funny to say, it wants to come out. Patience is not my greatest virtue, so this took work. Over the years, I needed to learn that thinking about my grocery list while someone was telling me about their life was not a good idea. Now I love to listen to people talk. But it took years of consistent work to get me here. If you are willing to do the work, you will actually find out other people are pretty cool.

Slowing down and being present, not only in conversation, but in all areas of life, offers us the opportunity to see life in a beautiful way. Imagine not worrying about work the next day while you were watching your child's hockey game. Or celebrating each success and joy in life as it passes, because you haven't already moved on to the next task you need to accomplish.

So many of us are in fast-track mode, jumping from one thing to the next without noticing what is passing by. Each day is the same: more hustle, more bustle, go go go. Others are barely seeing any joy at all. Feeling beaten down to a place where nothing matters anymore.

Disconnection is terrible for your sensuality. Sensuality is the pleasure of being present to all the magic as it passes you by. The amazing conversation with someone in a coffee shop. The best ice cream you have ever tried: Hagen-Daaz Peanut Butter and Chocolate from the tub. Each bite a delight on your tongue. You play with your kids, without thinking about work ... sometimes. When you decide to make the effort to be present in all things, as much as you can, it's the greatest joy you can experience.

When my client Kim and I were doing work in sacral week of The Chakra Business Academy, one of the hardest things she had to work through was being present. She went to all the networking events, but she did not want to be there. This resulted in her putting a mask on, going into Robot Kim mode, and taking a monster breath of relief when she finally got back home. There were no true connections made, because she wasn't fully there.

Our work that week was to find a way she could stand in her stardust, doing what she loved, and allow herself to shine. That meant finding what suited her abilities, and not just going some place she didn't want to be, pretending she wanted to be there. When she placed her energy where she felt called, she showed up completely. Within a week of our chat, she was booking clients and feeling completely present in what she was doing.

Feeling sadness

When your sacral has been turned right down, or even off, the feeling of disconnect from yourself and others can leave a deep sadness. It could be due to a situation you are going through, or because of something that did or did not happen in your life.

This chakra governs your ability to feel fully in your body: owning your life, oozing confidence, and trusting that you are fully supported and cared for. Obviously, if none of this is going on, you are left feeling hollow and vacant.

That is exactly how I felt when my son and I stopped speaking when he was 17. Things got to a point where it was toxic to be in each other's lives, and my health was at an all-time low. It was the hardest and most painful decision of my life, and it left me feeling empty, as though a piece of me had been ripped out. I was completely lost, and had no idea who I was anymore.

There was a huge hole where my sacral energy would have been. I spent my days curled up in a fetal position, getting up to work with clients, then going back to lying on the couch again. This all happened while I was supposed to be planning my wedding. It got to be too much. The over-whelm of wedding planning was suffocating me. What was supposed to be the happiest day of my life had me curled up behind my couch and crying on the floor. I eventually broke, and my husband and I ran off to Vegas.

I couldn't show up for anyone anymore, I could barely make it through the day. The crazy part was that no one knew how bad it was. I kept it very well-hidden. On the outside, I was a fortress; on the inside, I was a puddle. If you looked close enough, you could see the sadness leaking.

That was only two years ago. A lot has happened since then. I went into the sadness one person, and came out completely new. Before, I was content getting through my days. After, I was immersed in hearing Angels and doing chakra readings. Going deep into my darkness allowed the light to find me. If I hadn't felt that sadness, I don't know if my gifts would have appeared.

In truth, it wasn't until about five months ago that the sadness fully evaporated. I had convinced myself that I was feeling better, but I also wasn't fully showing up yet. That meant that when I made the decision that I wanted to have an online business that served people all over the world, I believed I could do it braless and with no make-up. I told myself that I was a hippie chick and all the right people would know that my message was true.

Then I read *The E-Myth Revisited*, and read a story about how a car salesman who was incredible but wore a brown suit sold less than the terrible salesman in the blue pinstripe suit. People only saw the suit, not what he was actually capable of doing.

That was my wake-up call. I realized that if spending five minutes a day on my make-up meant I would have a better opportunity to reach more people, I was committed. The more I put effort into myself, the more the sadness seemed to recede. My sacral was being turned on, the more I turned up.

This was also true for Jeanine when we started to work together. When I did her chakra reading, she was full of sadness, and negative self-talk. She couldn't believe I could read it. She explained that everyone thought she was always happy and in a good mood because that was what she showed. But inside, it was a completely different story. She felt alone, and was still holding onto something from her past that felt heavy and sad.

Together, we worked through releasing the pain. Jeanine found a beautiful space within her that was full of light. Today she shows up for her work, with make-up on, smiling and loving every second of serving others. She shows up with the story still inside her, but now she sees it as a beautiful way to connect with others, not a heaviness that holds her still.

Having a beautifully shining sacral chakra requires you to stand fully in the light of who you are. This means that you need to be fully open to loving your flaws. I believe that what you see as your weaknesses are actually your greatest strengths. What you think makes you unlovable is the very thing everyone loves about you.

This is the week in my program where the masks come off. Where you let go of the control you have been holding onto. It requires trust that you are still going to be safe without the walls. No one will step forward and hurt you. It is a gorgeous release of all sorts of emotions.

Shame, guilt and fear, all get sent away. In their wake is the freedom to see yourself, body and mind, as the beautiful vessel of love and light that you are. You were created in love and your body is a reflection of that. When you can feel that energy pulsing through your body, it awakens something within you. You shine. That glow is what people see and want to be around.

When you are fully present, radiating light, showing up for yourself and others, this will translate to abundance. You will find yourself being asked to speak, be interviewed, or to coach. The light within you becomes a magnet for others to be drawn to. There is no better feeling in the world than living in this space.

CHAPTER SIX

Cave of Wonders

SOLAR PLEXUS

Resistance:
Imposter syndrome
Energy:
Belief system in yourself
Characteristics:
I am heard
I am seen
I am worth it
I am enough
Side Effects:
My voice doesn't matter
Feeling invisible
I'm not good enough
I need to do more research/school/certifications

Goal of clearing this chakra: Taking serious action in creating a business you love because you are fricking awesome.

This is my favourite chakra to talk about. I call it the cave of wonders (totally a *Little Mermaid* reference), because when someone says something to us about who we are, it tends to get dumped in this chakra. From an early age, what our parents say, the kids at school say, your cranky grandpa yells, and everyone in between tells us forms a belief system about who we are, one that wasn't supposed to be ours.

You may have felt like you were to be seen, not heard. Talking was frowned upon. You were told to be quiet all the time. Or maybe you were just sent to your room or outside. Your parents didn't seem to want you around. When you were out at family events, the kids were told to go away. Sometimes, these feelings get stored in your solar plexus and you begin to believe your words don't matter. You stop trying.

You may have been a shining student, always paying attention in class, and still got comments that you could have done better. The sensation of needing to be "on" all the time, do the best, be the best. Or maybe the opposite was true. You didn't quite fit in with anyone and felt completely isolated from others. There didn't seem to be any crowd you connected with in school. You started to feel there was something wrong with you, that no one liked you.

And the list goes on. At any point, when someone makes a comment about our weight, the way we cook, how we dress, the colour of our hair, we have a split second to throw that thought away, or to make it part of our belief system in ourselves. If it becomes a belief, you toss it in the solar plexus, sometimes never going back to deal with that feeling.

I can tell when someone has been doing work on themselves, because when I read this chakra I can get right to the bottom of it and find the initial belief that was picked up as a kid. If someone is a hoarder of other people's ideas about themselves, I can't even get in. Either they present as a firmly closed door, or I get vertigo trying, the swirling of undealt emotions making me feel overwhelmed, dizzy, and nauseous.

The truth is, we will always have work to do in this area, even as we become successful entrepreneurs. Someone always has something to say. When you are committed to keeping this chakra clear, you learn to deal with the emotions faster. You learn the *toss and forget* method is a sure-fire route to crashing and burning. When your mission is big enough, you step up and do the tough stuff.

My voice doesn't matter

If there is one belief about myself that presented itself over and over again, it was this one. For most of my life, I was afraid to say the things I felt or thought because I didn't want to hurt anyone. Especially anyone I loved. When you live around depression, you take on a certain responsibility for your words. I've seen something I said cause a week (or more) of sadness for a loved one, and it sucks. I wouldn't even tell a fly to bugger off (OK, I totally would), but hurting someone I love is at the bottom of things I like to do in a day.

This trend of not speaking, being afraid my words, was a poison I carried for most of my life. The soft melody of "don't rock the boat" always playing in my subconscious. Whether at work, at play, or at home, I spun a tale of keeping the big stuff to myself. I became the queen of useless banter and talking about inappropriate things. That was way safer. Instead of my words being powerful enough to wound, I made sure that my words didn't matter at all.

Unfortunately, this was reflected in the types of guys I dated. A long string of poo heads entered my life. They ranged from the ones who stayed at my house, but tried to pick up other women when we went out (we weren't technically an item, so it was OK, right?) to guys who only wanted to date me until we got naked. I also dated an atheist, that one really took my voice away. Every relationship matched the pattern I had created in my belief system: what I said was worthless.

As I write this book I am getting challenged by each chakra as I go. I received a text from my ex while I was preparing this chapter. It was immediately combative and sent me into a major panic attack. I didn't feel I had done anything wrong, yet there I was, shaking away. Thoughts of *why* running through my head. Why does this man still have this effect on me? Why do I let him affect me this way? When will this not matter anymore? I spent the next morning meditating and going within. It was there that I realized he still held part of my voice. That I felt small and couldn't speak around him. Where I am the type to avoid confrontation, he begins with it. It took me most of the next morning, but I cleared out my solar plexus and was ready to serve my clients by lunch.

When I started working with Selena, she was going through the same thing. She stepped fully into her stardust knowing it was going to be a challenge. Her mission is to help women whose husbands suffer from mental illness learn to find themselves within their relationships so they can stay together and have even stronger connections.

I felt her pain when she spoke about not feeling like she could always tell her husband her thoughts out of fear of how he would react. I knew exactly what that felt like. We worked on opening her voice to include him. Allowing them to find a platform for them to grow in together. When she opened up and used her voice, magic happened in her home, and in her life.

Feeling invisible

I know this may come as a surprise to you all, but I was not popular in high school. I don't know if I watched too many TV shows that idealized the experience, but my version was sad. I mean like, I tried out for the cheerleading squad every year and never made it. Sad. With my anxiety, I believed everyone was talking about me in the halls, so I looked down. If I couldn't see them, they couldn't see me. That was my mantra.

I did, however, let my nerd flag fly pretty high. I was in all the school plays, did the announcements, and openly shared my feelings for Jordan Knight from New Kids on the Block. Yep. Cool vibes oozed out of me. The reason I loved anything with a stage or platform was because I didn't like myself enough to be myself. I needed to be a character, I felt better being hidden.

Most of my life I lived in the shadows. I didn't think I had what other people did, so I didn't try. When I started personal training, it was the first time in my life I actually liked who I was and didn't feel invisible. It was the first time other people saw me as being an expert and good at what I did. I loved it. I vowed then that I would only do jobs that made me feel empowered. Helping others became my jam.

Was there a time when you felt you weren't seen? It happens. Maybe you had a spiritual gift and you weren't allowed to talk about it. So you hid from your parents and started to feel isolated. This was what happened with my client Michelle. She was told she was never to discuss the things she felt, saw, or heard. Can you imagine being young and being told that what you felt or saw wasn't real? Even when it was? It left her feeling empty.

For years she remained silent and hidden. Taking jobs where she could be invisible. It was easier not to be seen, so she melted in with what was going on around her. You could have spent an afternoon talking to her, but years later, not remember her at all. This became her new gift. Being forgotten.

Working together has been such a beautiful journey of self-discovery for Michelle. She has been working every day at letting go of being invisible, and allowing her light to shine. She went from literally having a still from *The Invisible Woman* as her Facebook profile picture to sharing her story and stepping into her stardust. I still can't believe how beautiful the transformation has been.

I'm not good enough

This is a classic solar plexus gem. It plagues almost everyone I know, experienced or novice. The fear that what we do, say, or accomplish won't be able to help anyone. The words "what if" making our lives a miserable state of being paralyzed. Fear backs this big guy up. It's like steroids for not moving forward in life.

I know what I am about to write will make the grammar police show up at my door, but for the sake of the message I'm trying to make, I need to say it like this.

We pick up the feeling of not being *good enough* right away. We didn't clean the house *good enough*. We don't *do good* enough in school. We aren't *good enough* as girlfriends or boyfriends. It is a phrase expressed by both word and action that isn't meant to anchor into our cellular structure, but infects us anyway. As a parent, I see it happening in front of my eyes. I know that there are times when my kids look at me after something I have said and I think, "Uh oh, that went straight to the solar plexus."

I believe this thought secretly causes the most resistance in people. It can stop you from doing exactly what you are meant to do in the world. You get clear on what you want, you put your thoughts and energy into making it happen, and then boom. What if it doesn't work. What if I can't help them. What if I fail. What if I succeed. What if I suck balls. All the what ifs start dancing around your head like sugar plum fairies at Christmas time. These all boil down to one belief: I am not *good enough*.

I could drop my story and hundreds of others here. But instead I want to inspire you to ignore these what-if statements. They are the trappings of your current self, trying to keep you small and comfortable. It is the very reason most people give up before they get started. You 100 percent have everything within you right now to help others and to make a difference in the world. It takes courage and bravery to accept your resistance, love on it, and then bring it with you everywhere you go.

There are points in our life when imposter syndrome will rear its ugly head. Be brave. Be bold. Take it by the horns and let it know you are exactly where you need to be, doing exactly what you are meant to be doing. Take that resistance. One of the mottos in my program is FUCK OFF FEAR. Ain't no one got time for that!

I need to do more research/school/certifications

Speaking of imposter syndrome rearing its ugly head. This is another way it creeps up and makes us feel small, like we can't do what we are meant to. The answer can't be inside us... right? It must be found somewhere else. Like in a classroom, bookstore, or library. If I just take one more class I will be ready. This will be my last. Until the next one. And the next one.

It's one of the most beautiful distractions in the world. I can't even begin to tell you the amount of money I have spent on taking courses. Each one held the answer to a problem I had, or offered the solution I needed. I wouldn't go back and un-take any of them. I did find something magical in every one.

What I didn't realize until recently, however, was that even though I was learning from everything I was taking, I didn't think I could actually do the things that these people were doing. They had something I didn't. Whether they were better looking, better educated, had more reach, or knew more about business, I told myself that they could do what I wanted to do because they had more than me.

There is more than one client that I work with who feels she needs to have something else in place before she can get started. Whether it be a course, certification, or reading a book about it. I tell them all the same story. In February of 2017, I was given the message from my Angels that I could read chakras. It seemed a little far-fetched to me, but I was at a stage in my life where I had nothing better to do but trust. So, without researching chakras, or exploring what they meant, I asked people to let me practice on them.

There wasn't a soul I read who felt that their readings weren't bang on. I heard the gentle guidance in my head letting me know what to read, nudging me into each chakra to find the information. I can't explain it other than magic. That is what it felt like to me. There was only one day when I got in my ego brain and questioned what was happening. On that day I freaked out and wondered what was happening to me when I went in and out of energy all day. Was my brain melting? I went to bed filled with anxiety that night, but when I woke up, I had renewed my connection to Universe and knew everything was OK.

So many other things could have happened if I hadn't just believed what I received and trusted I could do it. If I felt I had needed to go learn all about chakras, or take another course about them or even read more books, I wouldn't be writing this book, and The Chakra Business Academy wouldn't exist.

You have everything, right now, right here, inside of you. The answer to who you are here to serve, and how you can find them. Not letting go of the fear that's holding you back is the only thing holding you back. Pun intended.

So how do you let go of the beliefs others have said to you over the years, collections of words and events sinking deep into your DNA? You rewrite your script. Overwrite the messages with new ones. Build a belief system you can grow with, become, love. No one should ever be able to take your voice away, or make you feel small. Instead of choosing fear, choose love. It is the answer to all of this.

Grab your journal right now and write out 10 "I am" statements. Positive ones! Like I am successful, I am wealthy, I am beautiful, I am free. Make these your new DNA statements. Look at them every day, read them out loud. If it seems ludicrous, don't do it. It's your journey. Find another way to change your thoughts.

Another incredible way to clear out the solar plexus is to write all the reasons why you *can* be awesome and have a successful business. Make a list of as many "I can" statements as you can! Again, loving the play on words here. Every time you try to tell yourself you can't do something, grab this list. Remember how you felt right now, when you told yourself you can.

The Care Bear Stare

THE HEART CHAKRA

Resistance:

Giving too much

Energy:

Heart pain

Heart heaviness

Inhale and exhale

Characteristics:

Open

Love

Caring

Support

Side Effects:

Exhausted

Heavy

Loneliness

G oal of getting this chakra cleared: Throwing love fearlessly out of your heart like a Care Bear winning a fight against No Heart and Beastly.

The heart chakra is my chakra. I am in a state of being love and spreading love to as many people as I can. Giving freely of your heart isn't always easy, and sometimes people aren't nice to it, but for me, it is the only option. Love is the only answer to our problems. To every act of violence. If we could connect as one global movement, spreading love like Care Bears, we could eradicate so much hate, which is what fear is.

Fear is the opposite of love. If you make the decision to stay small, fear helped you make that decision. If you stay home from a concert, fear held your hand in that decision. When you talk badly about someone in the office, fear is whispering in your ear. We all have fear. Even me. I am not perfect, and my fear tries very hard to win an argument sometimes. It is in those moments, when fear and love are fighting, that you have to pay close attention. In that moment, if you close your eyes and quiet the world around you, you will hear it. The sweet sound of your heart beat. The truest form of life as we know it. When you stop and listen to it, you will know you are love.

There are some really mean people in the world who don't treat hearts very nicely. They purposely hurt them with words and actions. It's totally cool not to like them by the way, but I believe, as daughters and sons of the light, that we can bring love even to the people we hate. That we give to all from our hearts, without taking in their toxic fear.

These people may have caused you to be extremely protective of your heart, for fear someone else will do hurtful things to you. You may get to a point where being alone is easier than giving your heart to someone. This doesn't help you, or the world, or the amazing humans who will treat your heart with the kindness and gentleness you deserve.

Learning to share your heart, but also to receive with it, is the key to having incredible relationships in both life and business. To me, your heart is your business card. You lead with love, and I want in with whatever you are doing. Hook me up! I want to surround myself with as much of that energy as I can. That is what's real. The rest is just an illusion created by fear.

Exhausted

Your heart is like lungs, it thrives on breathing. It inhales love, and it exhales love. When it inhales, it receives the love of others, abundance, peace, joy, and all the amazing things the world has to offer. When it exhales, it releases all that amazing energy back out into the world. As you draw in greatness, you are then able to breathe it back out to those you love and serve.

When you don't feel as though you deserve that greatness, you stop inhaling. You stop bringing beautiful things into your heart. If you have been hurt by too many people, your heart stops breathing all together. Afraid to bring in the wrong kind of energy, and petrified someone in the world will hurt its tender love if you breathe out.

When your heart chakra becomes distressed, or overly hurt, the most common way it responds is by becoming the martyr, or the nurturer. Instead of allowing in, you start to only give out. You distract yourself with the needs of others. Giving becomes your way of distracting yourself from the hurt you don't want to deal with. If Aunt Sue wants help moving, you are there to help pack boxes before the move and unpack them after. You find ways every day to help others. You become the person they call. Every day, whether it is a two-hour phone call with a friend or bringing someone to the doctors. When the day is over, you are exhausted. You look back and realize you didn't do anything for yourself.

In business, this shows up as always giving everything away for free. You feel terrible charging for helping others. It doesn't seem right. How can you serve if people can't afford you? Whenever someone needs you, you willingly share your knowledge with them, so they keep calling back. You become their saviour, they thank you, declaring they "wouldn't know what to do" if they didn't have you in their life. You absorb those words like a badge of honour, and then fall into bed bone-tired to fitful dreams that you can't remember in the morning.

This is your heart chakra out of whack. When you feel utterly exhausted each night, and every morning feels heavy, chances are you are having trouble receiving to your heart. This is very important in both life and business, because it means you are living externally. You choose caring about your husband, kids, and neighbours before caring for yourself. I'm going to guess that inside that heart of yours is something that you are trying to avoid. I get it. Sometimes not feeling the pain of a breakup or a loss of a loved one is easier. Eventually it needs care though. If it doesn't, the wound gets stored. I read it as scar tissue behind the heart. It stays there like a living energy source, drawing from your heart, causing pain.

When you allow yourself to feel out the pain, as hard as it may be, you open the air vent of your heart. It creates a place, where movement in and out can happen. One of the things I teach is being in a space of receiving through love. Some people find this concept hard in the beginning to understand, but it is the key to your success and those you are here to serve.

When someone needs your help, there needs to be an energy exchange between them and the Universe for the outcome to be realized. When someone pays for your service, they are making a declaration to the Universe that they are ready. They have a problem, and want a solution. You being in a state to receive allows that exchange to occur. This is a huge inhale into your heart. As you work with them, you exhale all the magic you can into what you are doing with them, moving them to the beautiful place the two of you have declared for them. It's a magical journey for both of you.

If you are not in a place to receive, there are two possible ways this will go. One, you will give them the answer without the monetary exchange, which means they will not get to the outcome because the Universe doesn't get involved.

Or two, the person will want the outcome enough to take their money elsewhere. You are such a beautiful soul, and you can't guarantee that the person they take their money to will give them the same love you would.

In life, you see this exchange in other ways. If you help move someone, and they offer to buy you dinner, or bake you a pie, in this way the heart remains open to bringing in love, so it can share love. If I do chakra readings, and I don't offer to work with someone, they might write a review, or post about their feelings. This keeps the flow of energy in and energy out.

This was a hard pill for my client Rebecca to swallow. She had been giving her services away for a long time, so when we began to work together, she did not believe that charging was the answer. For years, she had been over-tired and overwhelmed, and her business wasn't moving anywhere. The first couple weeks she was a little skeptical about receiving in to her heart. She communicated with her tribe, but didn't offer to work with them. She still found herself wanting to give them the answers, which was actually a disservice to them.

About three weeks in, she felt it. She felt the inhale into her heart and the air vent opened. Everything clicked into place. All those years, she had not been helping by giving everything away. All the people who didn't get the results because she felt weird taking the energy exchange they were making with the Universe. If I could make the sounds of birds chirping and sun shining right here I would, because that is what this revelation felt like to her. It was an awakening. She was able to receive FOR them, so they could achieve their greatness, and she could exhale all the love from her heart for their journey.

Heaviness

Chances are if you have picked up this book, you have the capacity to care too much. You hurt for all of humanity, animals, and the planet. The pain in the world, feels like your pain. It can be overwhelming, the weight crushing down on you. How can things be so bad? How can you make it better?

What happens over time is that without protecting yourself, you collect all this pain in your heart. It begins to weigh you down like a sponge filling with water. Sometimes the water in your heart even spills out your eyes. You find yourself emotional over everything. It becomes unbearable to see or hear anything anymore.

When your heart is heavy, going out becomes more difficult. Being around people, feeling their pain, it just wants to add to your already growing chest pain. Taking deep breaths becomes difficult. There is no more room in your heart to store anyone else's hurt. Our human bodies weren't made for this much.

You are a gift to this Earth. Not everyone carries the ability to feel on this level. There are some important self-care tips to keep your heart from collapsing under this pressure. One is to give away the hurts of others to something bigger than you. Think about it. Up above us, high in the sky, is Universal love. It is massive and is here to support those in need. That is why we pray, meditate, and release to it. It has the capacity to be never-ending, full of love, and there for us whenever we need it. This beautiful energy source is far more capable of holding space for the people who are hurting than we are. Trust that if you ask for love or support for someone, it will be there.

I had to trust God to take care of my son when Ethan chose to live on the streets over seeking help and coming home. For days I cried. For days I could feel the weight in my heart suffocating me. Then, one day as I lay curled in my chair, I heard His voice in my head, "Give me your worry and I will take care of your son." I released all my fears to Him. I knew that endless loving energy in the sky would be my eyes and ears. I trusted that they were far more capable of looking after Ethan than I was.

This might seem daunting and scary, but there needs to be room to receive in your heart. If it is too full, there will be no inhale available. Slowly take one thing out at a time, and give it away. If you are feeling motivated, give it all away. Don't make this harder than it is. Sit quietly with your eyes open or closed. Feel the pain in your heart. Ask for who you believe in to come and ease the pain. If you are able to see the feelings being removed from your heart, whether as a ball in your hands, or a wisp in the air, great. If not, it doesn't matter. Trust that the Universe wants to take this from you, and let go of the burdens you are carrying.

Loneliness

There are some people in this world who aren't very nice. They live in the fear world, not the love world. These people may have taken your heart and not given it the attention and love it deserved. They may have said mean things, done terrible things, or even shut you out. This can make your heart fearful of giving it love vibes out to everyone it meets.

It may feel scary to go all in with your heart, and if someone has taken advantage of your awesomeness, you may want to close the heart shop up for good, board the windows, and place the "no solicitors" sign up outside. This space can feel lonely, like there is no one who understands what you are going through or what you feel.

But what if there was a way to open yourself up to receive and spread love, without the fear of it getting hurt again? To freely go "all in" when you meet a new friend or romantic partner? Your heart vibes will roll out of you like laughter from Santa at Christmas. The first few times you do it, it might feel scary, but when you get used to stepping out of your comfort zone, it becomes the happiest feeling there is.

The way to unlocking your heart and spreading joy in the world is to ask for help. Not from anyone you know, not even from me. You ask for help from the Universe. When you wake up in the morning, ask the Universe to only bring good people into your life who will treat your heart with kindness. Know that by asking for these people, the Universe will meet you in these thoughts, and bring kind, loving people into your life.

If you are wondering if it can be that easy. Why can't it? After doing the work from the last few chapters, opening up and releasing fear, it should come a bit easier. There is nothing to lose here, but definitely love to gain!

Your heart is such a magical piece to your energetic puzzle. Filling it with good thoughts and good intentions keeps it full. Imagine it like your body's gas tank. A really great way to fill it up is to focus on all the good you have in your life. Have you ever written a gratitude journal? Every morning when I wake up, I have a daily practice that includes writing out at least three things I am grateful for. It could be fresh coffee, sunsets, new clients, my husband and kids. Every morning I write these things, it's like inserting the nozzle of gratitude into my heart, and filling the tank with love.

There is so much to be grateful for. If you take the time to let the things that aren't serving you out, you will create the space to inhale all the amazing things the world has to offer. When you know you are worthy of love, you can't help but see it everywhere. There is no other answer.

CHAPTER EIGHT

Know Your
Super Power

THROAT CHAKRA

Resistance:

Illness

Energy:

Voice

Written Word

Characteristics:

Freedom

Connect

Serve

Share

Side Effects:

Clenched jaw/teeth

Weight on your chest

Lack of motivation

Goal of clearing this chakra: To get your voice back from Ursula, like Ariel in *The Little Mermaid*

This chakra is extremely powerful in getting your message out into the world. It is your vehicle for change. Whether your voice or your written word is your superpower, the important thing is to use it to make a difference.

The throat chakra just happens to be tied very heavily with the lower chakras. That means, if your root, sacral or solar plexus is out, chances are your throat feels it. When you are afraid of the judgment of others, are a people pleaser, or believe your words don't matter, your voice takes the hit. You keep your words to yourself, because who cares anyway. Then, when your voice is gone, everything else seems unimportant. You go into "why bother" mode, which feels like a catatonic zombie state. This is the last place you want your throat chakra to get to. Once it hits this level, often illness is next. You may find yourself with thyroid problems, or chronic sinusitis.

On a smaller scale, when you are fighting your message, you can get sick. I mean fever, flu, massive cold sick. I spoke to two clients today who were suffering from this exact fear. One was curled up in a blanket on the floor like a sushi roll. For months she has been working on finding her message and getting it out in to the world. She had posted some amazing things on Facebook, there were people connecting with her, and then boom, she got sick. The thought of speaking to potential clients and getting herself out there made her physically sick.

Another client has been fighting illness for years, but recently has been having severe colds. She asked me what was going on, and when I read her energy, it was directly correlated to her solar plexus and believing what she was offering to the world wasn't good enough. I could feel her doubts hundreds of miles away. As she was creating amazing course material to make a huge impact to those she serves, her old belief patterns from childhood reared their ugly head, and down she went.

Think of all the times you were working in a job you hated. Your boss sucked, you weren't appreciated, going in felt like it was sucking the life out of you. Every morning was painful. Eventually you gave up saying anything because no one was listening and it didn't matter anymore. Now think of how many times you were sick while you were there. Coincidence? I think not!

Clenched jaw/teeth

When you are holding back things you want to say to someone, you can end up clenching your teeth or jaw so tight it hurts. It's like a bad case of biting your tongue. You may be fighting with a loved one or someone at work, but you aren't speaking your truth, so you clench. When you do it for months, you can begin to grind in your sleep or cause pain in your neck or ears.

Nothing good comes from keeping how you feel bottled up. There are times when saying things may be inappropriate, like when someone is on the toilet, or at Aunt Mary's

50th birthday bash. But finding a time when the person you need to speak to is feeling calm and releasing what you feel is super awesome. Words are one of the powerful expressions in the world, so holding them in isn't good for anyone. This holds true for when you are on the receiving end, as well. Even when I don't agree with what someone is saying to me, I honour that it meant a lot to them, that feelings are important.

When you lose your ability to express your words, you may begin to lose other pieces of yourself along the way. It starts by you giving up your favourite show. Then you stop suggesting things you like to do. Maybe you even give up your spirituality (been there). Piece by piece, little parts of you disappear. It's like the words you stopped speaking were just the beginning. As each day you don't express yourself passes, the words you swallow take more of you away. Sometimes holding it all in not only clenches your teeth, it makes you furious. Snapping at your family or coworkers becomes the norm. You feel angry all the time and you don't know why. The unspoken thoughts become a fire in your belly.

A good way to begin to let these feelings out is by journaling. I know you've probably heard this before, and you may think it's a load of hokey, but getting the energy you are holding inside you out is good on so many levels. Each word written on the page is one less that will explode out later. The pressure in your teeth and jaws isn't going to get better on its own. A little support from you will help tremendously.

Weight on your chest

Carrying your words inside without letting them out can feel like you are carrying the weight of the world. Unexpressed thoughts sitting on your chest, making it difficult to breathe. You can't remember the last time you felt like you took a deep breath. Sometimes you feel like you are suffocating. The weight can feel crushing.

This can be over so many things. You know something about someone you care about and are told to keep it a secret. You have decided not to tell people that you found a lump in your breast and you try to deal with it alone. Something terrible happens to you and you don't know where to turn. You want to leave your relationship and are lost on how to do it. Each of these are just a few examples of ways in which you carry something you need to get off your chest.

There is nothing more crushing than knowing you need to do something but holding it in. It forces you into a state of limbo. Your future and life pause. There is no movement. Life feels stagnant and you stop caring. When you get here, in either life or business, it is important to keep some flow of trajectory. Movement toward something. If you let the water settle and pool, that's when you feel like you may drown. Any small step forward is movement. That means you could write a to-do list, talk to a friend, reach out to a therapist, meditate. The idea is that you release some pressure off your chest. When you count up the movement of many small steps, you cross an entire ocean. Keep yourself moving.

Lack of motivation

Your voice and words are powerful. Everything you say means something to you. When you don't let the flow of your purpose out, feeling de-motivated is the response. Stardust is some potent stuff, holding it in is super uncomfortable.

Let's say you have been with your partner for many years. Over the course of your relationship, your voice has slowly left you. There is no compromise, your words don't matter. Day by day you feel less inclined to show up. What's the point in trying? Nothing you say matters anymore. The feeling you have in your house starts to spread out to all areas of your life. A little pocket of you disappears. This goes on until one day you snap. All the years of pent-up words come flowing out. You can't do this anymore, your voice is freed.

This was not only my story, but my client Cara's as well. For more years than she could count, Cara had been living a life where nothing she said was heard. She slowly stopped talking. Day by day she became less interested in what was going on around her. Day by day she lost her motivation.

This not only affected her relationship, it affected her life. She lost her motivation. She had built a beautiful program. Actually downloaded it from Source energy, and had no desire to get it out.

When we started working together to get her incredible gift out into the world, she had trouble with talking to people. It took months for her to get someone on the phone. Cara had lost not only her voice, she had lost the piece of her that held her confidence.

For all three of the women that I talk about on this chapter, their voices had been taken by someone in their lives. Whether it was family, their partner, or life circumstances, Ursula the witch had come and taken their voice (*Little Mermaid* reference).

As in the movie, it is possible to win the fight and gain your voice back. You need to be able to stand up for things that matter, even if it is just to watch *So You Think You Can Dance*, or watching Christmas movies in November. What you like to do, what you enjoy, matters.

When you begin to speak about who you are, momentum gains, like a tiny snowball at the top of a hill, getting bigger as it travels down. As you unlock your voice, your message becomes clearer, you remember your purpose. Like the end of *The Little Mermaid* when the shell breaks at Ariel's feet and slowly the blue cloud raises up to her throat until she can sing again.

Sometimes speaking to friends and even professionals helps get your voice moving. I have a wonderful psychologist in my life who has helped me find my voice again. Journaling is also amazing. Taking the words that have been trapped inside and getting them out. When the clutter of day-to-day, bottled-up thoughts, feelings, and emotions is removed, that's when you can spread the message of your stardust.

CHAPTER NINE

Trust

THIRD EYE

Resistance:
Sleeping
Energy:
Belief in something bigger
Characteristics:
Peace of mind
Content
Connected
Side effects:
Stress
Anxiety
Trouble keeping your eyes open

Goal of getting this chakra cleared: A knowing deep inside that everything is going to be ok.

This chakra is the secret to all things magical and successful. It is where you get to release your fears and live in peace. I can hear Bob Marley in my head as I type this. "Don't worry... about a thing. Cause every little thing gonna be alright." When you can connect to the fact that there is a beautiful energy all around you, wrapping you up in a warm, safe blanket, you realize you don't have to do everything alone.

For most of my life I knew there was something. I was baptized and confirmed Anglican, however, I am not one to sit still for any length of time, so church was not my jam. I loved Sunday school A LOT. Give me some crafting supplies and colouring, and I was good for hours. When I was in my early 20s, I found Goddess energy and could have spent all day, every day skipping in the forest stoned, my spiritual sisters and I finding quiet corners by the lake to do our cards and soak in the powers below. Clearly this was not something I could keep up with forever.

Enter the eight-year relationship with an atheist. I'll call this the *unravelling*. The time when I forgot who I was, what I wanted, and where my voice went. I could have kept my spirituality going, if I had been strong enough. This is not his fault by any means. These years were meant to be part of the bigger picture journey. I believe if I hadn't lost myself so deeply, coming home wouldn't have felt so good. The minute we broke up, I put an altar beside my bed full of cards and crystals. When my husband Jeff and I got together, I was petrified he would run the other way when he saw it. I suppose putting it in the bedroom was the best choice – he really wasn't thinking about the altar when he made it to my bedroom (wink wink).

The real unveiling of my spirituality happened when I went to see my therapist one day. I had been seeing her on and off for ten years, but in this session something shifted. I was explaining to her that when my son Ethan and I broke up (cut ties from each other), I needed to do something that would help me feel better. I honestly would have tried anything. The darkness and sadness was so overwhelming. So, in my desperation I reached to meditating. For months I would YouTube what I thought I needed, and every day I would meditate. The first month was pure bliss as I slept through almost every single one. Over time I stayed awake, and eventually I started to hear Angels. As I was telling her this story, she began nodding. The next few words would change the course of my life forever. She told me she believed it was time. Ummmm... time for what? She said it was time for me to join *A Course in Miracles*.

I won't lie, I felt like I had made it into some secret society because I had never heard of this before, and after seeing my therapist for ten years, I finally made it in. I showed up for the first class, nervous and excited, only to be told nothing in life was real. First thought, maybe I wasn't ready. Second thought, there are only two choices, love or fear. I choose love.

Stress

Stress is the polar opposite of feeling like everything is going to be OK. Stress is the mistress who gets invited into the bedroom and who wants to be frisky all night long. You toss and turn, trying to push her away, but she keeps wanting to play. "How are you going to pay the bills this month?" "Who do you think you are?" "Why is Jane Doe saying things to people that aren't true?"

When you wake up in the morning, she runs her nails gently down your back, inviting you to come back to bed. "Lie down, you're tired," she says. "You don't actually want to get up right now. Come lay with me again. We can worry together. You don't have to be alone."

When you choose to get out of bed, ignoring her sweet callings, you don't find the day much better. It's as though everything that could go wrong does. This is the time you spill the coffee beans all over. The dogs start eating it off the floor, and you just know that this is not going to be good. You go to the fridge and you are out of milk. Now your coffee is going to suck.

It's 7 a.m. and your phone starts to ring. You look down to the 1-877 number and remember you haven't paid the phone bill yet this month. Not only does your coffee suck, your dogs are freaking out, and you are worried about money. Bring it on, day, what else do you have for me?!

The car won't start, the dog poops in the house, and you sit down in defeat on the ground. Why would the Universe do this to you? What did you ever do to deserve this? You are a good person.

Energy is the most beautiful gift in the world – and it is the most tragic gift in the world. The key to its success is in your third eye, your thoughts. When you bring all your awareness to what is going wrong around you, making mountains out of molehills, the Universe thinks that you want more of those things. Energy flows where belief and thoughts go.

I spent an incredible amount of time trying to shift my thinking to match what I wanted out of life. It was the most difficult thing, until it became easy. Years of reading *The Secret*, talking to the Universe, meditating, writing in my journal, feeling like nothing good was happening. I still walked around wearing stress like a suit of armor. Even though I believed all these things were possible, that I could have money, that I could serve people, that I could find joy, they eluded me.

It's one thing to believe things are possible. It is another to trust that it is happening. You hear phrases like, "release it to the Universe," or "give it to God, and know it is coming," and it feels like bullsnot. How do you think something and not stress about its outcome? If you are starting a new business, how does the overwhelming fear that it won't work not consume you? There are so many things that could go wrong.

Boom. There is the problem. There is no wrong. There is only movement. Decisions are taking steps to achieve an outcome. Each step that you take is one in the right direction because you are actually moving. This is the beginning of you and the Universe speaking the same language.

When your energy shifts into one of decision and movement, the Universe shifts with you. When you take a step, any step forward, you declare you are ready to achieve the outcome. You start to receive phone calls, or meet new people who have the skills you require, you start to feel like things are going your way.

This means removing the fears that cause the stress. Fear is the nastiest destroyer of all things good, and doesn't really exist. When you are feeling the fear that causes the stress, it is usually over something that hasn't even happened yet. For example, you are completely unhappy in your job and want to leave it. It is sucking the joy out of your soul. Instead of walking into work and saying *see ya*, you stress about how your parents will feel about the decision, what will happen financially, and if you will end up living on the streets. All of this does not exist. Your parents may be thrilled to see you happy, you might land the job of your dreams, and move to your dream apartment. You stop yourself from doing things based on illusion.

Anxiety

Leveling up from stress is anxiety. I am one of the most anxious people in the world. Small things can set me off, and I'm shaking like a leaf for hours. It has been a long, confusing relationship between us, me and anxiety. For years I would try to stuff her back down. Every time I would feel anxious about something someone said, leaving my house, or moving into a new version of myself, I would run back into my comfort zone and hide.

Clearly anxiety was there to tell me that this was a bad decision. I would hear ringing in my head and the words "abort mission, abort mission." Who was I to argue with that? My worst panic attack was driving home from a job I hated. I kept seeing myself getting in an accident over and over again. My hands tightened on the wheel, my breathing went fast and hard, and I thought I was going to die. Even as I type this, I can vividly replay the vision of my car hitting another car and crashing over the guardrail. It was ten minutes of the same movie reel playing over and over in my head. I drove right to a health food store, shaking, and asked them to help me. The woman that worked there must have thought I was crazy. I left with chewable tablets for immediate relief and some St. John's Wort.

The problem with anxiety is that it stems from fear. Fear is false, and it is the opposite of love. My anxiety shows up when I am afraid of what something looks like. It's change. If I can't see what the change is, my anxiety says change is bad. But how do I know that change is bad? What if the decision I make to head into the unknown is good, or even great? When anxiety is driving, I am not connected to my third eye. I turn off the GPS and let anxiety take the wheel. Generally, this leads to her driving me back to the same place where I started. Usually that means we pull back into the driveway, allowing me to stay safe.

Today, anxiety is my superpower. I know that when I am feeling it, on the other side is greatness. This helps me lean into the discomfort. I've learned to invite anxiety on the drive with me. It's coming anyway, it's just a matter of who is in the driver's seat. And to be honest, I was getting tired of going in circles back to my own driveway. It was time for a change of scenery. Road trip time to Awesomeville, where all your dreams CAN come true!

Trouble keeping your eyes open

So when amazing guidance comes flying into your brain from Source energy and you don't want to listen, it's like there is an invisible hand that wants to shut your eyelids. You could be hearing that you could make loads of cash by working from home, and the information will be too much for you to handle, so you start to yawn and yawn, then your eyes will shut without you having any control over it.

Then there is the issue of you moving forward in your business and being afraid. You make yourself a tea, get comfy in front of your computer, and boom, you feel overwhelmingly tired. Maybe a nap would be better. If you napped, you could feel more energetic and could get more done. But somehow you feel more tired when you wake up than you did when you lay down.

It feels like every time you go to do anything that has to do with business, you feel like sleeping. You go to watch a video online and start yawning. You talk to your partner over dinner and want to close your eyes. The thought of listening to the guidance and trusting yourself seems like the silliest idea ever, since you only want to sleep.

I have an incredible client who, every time we talk, yawns. For one hour straight, she looks as though I am putting her to sleep. She is deeply connected and knows exactly what is going on. It's her way of absorbing information, but it still shows up as wanting to fall asleep.

When the Universe and you are in a great conversation, your third eye remains open and information flows freely in to guide you. It's like when I downloaded that I could read chakras. There was a split second where I questioned how that could even be possible since I never studied them, but then I just accepted it and said, "OK, guess I should practice."

Fighting guidance is exhausting. It's like digging your heels in when someone offers to take your hand and lead you in the direction of greatness. I see an insolent child, pulling away from something amazing, stomping their feet and saying, "No, I don't want to go!" Inside, you have a super amazing dream team of support that will take all your cares and worries away, allowing you to focus on what lights you up. It's free, easy to use, and requires only trust.

Giving away fear and trusting that you are going to be OK seems impossible, until it is possible. I understand this now. Before I learned to trust that nothing bad was going to happen, I got stressed and nervous about everything. When something bad happened, I would think, "Why is this happening to me?" Everything felt like an attack, like I had done something wrong. When you trust with your third eye, it changes the way you see things. I now ask,

"When this happened, what was the lesson I needed to learn?" Things now happen for me. Instead of closing up my connection to trust, I open it to receive messages in any form they need to come.

CHAPTER TEN

Show Me The Money

CROWN CHAKRA

Resistance*:*
Calling crap to you
Energy*:*
Receiving
Characteristics*:*
Abundant
Successful
Flow
Side effects*:*
Stagnant
Unappreciated
Lack

Goal of getting this chakra cleared: Rocking a successful business you love

This is it! We've made it to the very top of your chakras, to the place where you can begin to call in all the good stuff the Universe has to offer. If you have been letting go of what hasn't been serving you along the way in each chapter, by now you are an open vessel of love and light, ready to bring magic to your life and business.

The crown is your drive-through window to Source energy. Opening yourself up there is like rolling down the window of your car and asking God to bring you whatever you would like. If you want abundance, ask for it – the important thing is to be specific. Saying, "I want abundance," could be read as finding a dime on the sidewalk. Ask for the amount, and when you want it by. Every first of the month, I declare the amount of money I would like to make that month. I am specific, I have a day I would like it by, and on average, it is delivered. This isn't by a stork or UPS. I have to work for it, but the work I do lights me up, so even if I have a couple things to do on a weekend, I feel connected and lit up while doing it. It helps that I can stay in my pjs, too.

What are all the things you want, have you thought about that yet? Does it still feel selfish? If it does, I'm guessing you read right through the book without doing the exercises. Writing things out makes them so much clearer and real. Even if you don't read the book again, just drift back and do the small shifting exercises that each chapter asks you to do.

For this chapter, I want you to open your mind to the idea of zero limits. That everything in the world is just as accessible to you as it is to Richard Branson and Oprah Winfrey. You do know they started off just like you: one person with a dream to make a difference.

Answer me this: If money was no object, what would you do? Personally, I would be jumping on a plane to Scotland. I may or may not come back. First class straight to my very own castle. Overlooking water. Where the staff wears kilts. And that is just the beginning! I would buy a big cottage on the lake where I could run retreats. I would take my children to Atlantis. I would remodel my house.

Money is energy, just like the pulling of two people together, or the synchronicity of thinking about a person and they call. Everything is always moving toward something or away from something. At this point, I hope you are all moving toward the place where you can clear out all the things that aren't serving your chakras, to call in serving your tribe from home, or in an office space.

Fighting away from these things, your stardust, your joy, feel icky and terrible. That is the last place I want for you. It means that your crown chakra is closed, no breath is coming into your heart, and chances are you feel like nothing good ever happens to you. Just one bad thing after another. Let's look at why this is happening.

Stagnant

Think of your body as a beautiful vase, and the energy you receive from your crown chakra as water pouring into your vase. Now plant an incredible bouquet of your favourite flowers in your energy. Mine are Gerbera daisies. My vase of life is brimming with orange, yellow, and pink flowers. When you are filling your vase with fresh energy water every day, the flowers flourish and grow. You can give them away to people and make them happy because there is an endless supply of beautiful flowers to pull from. If you shut down your crown and take no water energy in, the flowers wilt away. Harsh, I know. But think about this. You stop bringing life energy in. What happens to a vase of flowers when you don't change the water? The water goes stagnant, the flowers can't grow, and everything dies.

Your body feels the same way when you don't allow life force energy to come in through your crown, down to your heart, and out into the world. It forces you to feel stuck, paralyzed, and in limbo. Nothing moves through you. Nothing feels good. There is no flow.

When you live in fear, you may believe that if you open your crown, bad things will come in. I used to believe that too, and guess what? Bad things did enter. I called all sorts of terrible things to myself. Now I know to order exactly what I want. I open the crown window to the drive-through of the Universe and ask that only people I can serve enter my day, and to fill my home, street, and city block with all the happy people. That way no matter where I am, I converse and share space with the most amazing people.

I asked my husband to take the kids to the cottage for a few days so I could write my book. It was great, but at the same time lonely. I'm lucky to have found the guy that I could spend every waking hour with. When it came time for him to come home, I was so excited. I mapped out when he left the cottage and how long it would take for him to get home. I couldn't wait to have him back. Just knowing he is in the house when I am working makes me feel cozy.

He got home: enter the storm cloud of 2017. I didn't recognize who was in front of me. No kiss hello. Then a replay of how terrible the drive was and how nothing had gone right all day. Blah blah blah. I sat there in silence. What had happened to my husband? Then it got worse. Like way worse. The basement flooded with stinky, poopy water. He spent the rest of the evening standing in shit. Eventually he threw in the towel and went to bed. Unfortunately he woke up in the same mood, so enter a live bird in the house that the cats dragged in. One after another, terrible events kept happening as he brooded on the fact that terrible things kept happening.

Luckily, or maybe unlucky for him, he lives with me. I immediately went into "why are you calling all this to you, let's figure it out" mode. It came out that he hadn't been feeling like things were going well for weeks. He felt stagnant. So when one bad thing happened, it felt like that was just the way life was going to be, which only called more crap (literally) to him. By midday we had moved his energy and things got better, but wowzers, that was quite a roll.

This happens in business when you don't allow the good to flow in. This happened to Hank. For four years he tried to bring his business to a place of growth, but didn't realize he had closed his crown. He closed himself off because he didn't want anyone to know that he wasn't succeeding. The more time passed, the more he wanted to hide. This meant that his business was stuck. There was no movement. What changed? He reached out to receive a chakra reading. When I knew I could help solve his problem with him, he joined The Chakra Business Academy to receive guidance. He opened himself up emotionally and received kind words and support. Slowly but surely, his crown opened to all the amazing things the world had to offer his business, and his business mirrored that. People, abundance, clients, and support, all came flowing in his direction.

Unappreciated

Let me just put my hand up and say guilty here. When I give a ton of support to someone and they don't reciprocate with anything, even a thank you, I feel completely let down. It begins a cycle of thoughts about why no one appreciates anything I do. This thought is one that plagued me for many years, especially in my peak victim mode.

When your air vent of receiving and giving is rocking and in full swing, beautiful messages and gifts flow in, and love and light flow out. If you begin to feel as though all you do is give, there comes a point where your energy can't keep up. Like we talked about in the heart chakra, you exhale so much that you shut down. You get tired. In this tired state, it feels like nothing you ever do is good enough and no one appreciates what you do, so why do it anyway. The minute this thought pops in to your head, the door to good shuts.

The key here is to know your own boundaries. Be aware of how much you are giving so you don't get to a place of un-appreciation. Notice the small things that come back to you. This is a big one. Someone may not say thank you or perform a big act of gratitude, but have they spread the word about you or your service? They may be your biggest fan and you just don't know it.

In business it's so easy to give. This person needs help and they have no money. That person just wants some advice. I'm a spiritual person, we don't charge. All this is nonsense and doesn't help anyone. The person you help doesn't get the solution and you end up with an empty cup. You can only do this so much before you realize it's not healthy for you or them.

When I started working with Rhonda, she was the poster child for feeling this way. She didn't dare charge, people in need couldn't afford it. When I suggested she reach out and connect with people who I could see needed her, she felt as though she was invading their privacy. She had a bad case of the givesies. It only took a couple sessions to show her how giving without receiving did not help her or her client. Within a couple weeks she knew charging for her service meant her client made an energetic exchange with the Universe and would get the result. That being in the space to receive in order for that to happen was actually magical. Who doesn't like magic?!

Lack

People don't have money to pay for my services. Lack. I live in an area where people don't pay money for this. Lack. This is something that is hard to sell. Lack. I can't afford it. Lack. Each of these statements come from a place of fear. There is enough money in the world to do anything and go anywhere. We were taught as kids that life is hard and there was never any money. But what if that was a lie?

This is a hard pill to swallow, I know. But in order to be successful in business, you need to receive. So holding space for thoughts about there not being enough will quickly kill your dreams before you even get started. When you begin with thoughts about how hard it is going to be, and how no one will have any money, that is exactly where you will stay. When you begin with the knowledge that you need to receive for your clients to get the results, and you will hold space for them to do that, your business grows quickly.

I know this because I had an unsuccessful business for years because I believed that my city was in a recession and I couldn't change my prices. I wanted to be affordable for everyone. That meant I needed to work harder for less. I spent lots of money taking courses trying to figure out how to change that for myself. It wasn't until a very special mentor, Angela, explained that we needed to receive in order to serve. A light went off in me and the Universe. The day I heard that, my crown sighed and my business soared. And the people I work with – holy crap, do they do amazing things now.

We receive that which we think about. The more you think about lack, the more lack you will have. The more you believe that you can have all the money, the more money you will have. This does not make you selfish, or a bad person. It makes you a vessel for something bigger than you. It means you can help fulfill people's dreams and use this money to make major changes in the world. You can't give to charities if you don't have the money to give.

So how do you change how you think about money or the lack thereof? You begin by opening up to the idea that you can have it all. Write out all the things you would do with money. What would you buy? Where would you go? Would you leave your kids or take your friends? Make mental pictures of how you can change the world with money. Which charities would you support? How much do you want to give them? Imagine and write as much detail as you can.

Focus on calling this to you. That means opening up your crown and trusting that you can call in the good without taking in the bad. When something happens that sucks, know that there is something you needed to learn, but that it does not mean you are doomed to life of misery and shame. Ask the Universe to bring you clients, and not just any clients, all the good clients. You want the ones who will show up and do the work and are super fun to work with. Only those ones. Be clear. Allow the Universe to bring this to you. It might take more than 24 hours. Be patient. Trust that it is happening. That's the secret. Now you know it. Now you can do this.

CHAPTER ELEVEN

Stardust Maintenance

L iving in your stardust is magical. It can feel like rainbows, sunshine, and unicorns, all day, every day. Keeping the flow requires you to stay present in your body. That means you need to be aware of what is going inside your own body, and not get distracted by what is going on with everyone else's. The minute you leave your energy and go on a road trip to someone else's, you lose connection to all the good radio stations. It's like one minute you are car dancing, singing at the top of your lungs, and the next all you hear is the droning hum of white noise. One second your energy is up. The next it's way down.

Energy is not a stable thing. It ebbs and flows. High tides and low tides. Learning to hear your body cues before it sets off the trip wires of your chakras can make life a much more pleasant experience.

For example, if you know every time you go to Aunt Mae's house for family dinner that someone always says something about your weight, create a protective bubble around yourself so that the words bounce away from you and don't sink into your belief system about yourself (solar plexus).

The Universe thought it would be funny to shake up all areas of my chakras while I wrote each chapter of this book. As I anchored into feeling each chakra, I was forced to have to deal with something that required me to clear things. I am letting you know this because once a chakra is cleared, it doesn't mean it stays this way forever. Life throws curve balls all the time. You need to know when to duck before they hit you in the face, or worse, right between the legs.

How you do this is by noticing your moods, your triggers, and how you are reacting. For example, I'll tell you my least favourite curve ball while I was writing this book. As I was gearing up to write the solar plexus chapter, I took an evening off. Since my eyes didn't want to see text, Jeff and I were chilling and watching Netflix. As we were relaxing, catching up on some *Brooklyn 99*, my phone buzzed. It was late, after 11, well past when I normally stayed up, but I glanced down to see who it was.

Instant panic attack. My ex doesn't start conversations softly, and so I looked down to a very combative text. There were lots of accusing and argumentative statements. As I engaged, wave after wave of panic consumed me.

By the time I was done, my teeth were chattering, my body was shaking and I felt completely disassociated from myself. What just happened? Why was I responding so violently? I went to bed that night still panicking and woke up feeling off. I kept asking myself, "At what point do I take my power back? At what point does what he say not affect me?"

And then it hit me. I was feeling this way because while I was with him I didn't feel like I had a voice. My thoughts and feelings didn't matter. I was reliving how it felt when my solar plexus was completely out of whack. I spent the morning in meditation, giving away the belief that my words didn't matter. I did this so I could let go of his crap and I could show up for my clients.

There were so many lessons for me while writing this book. I was asked to reconnect to my feminine side, to learn to trust again, and to release all the things I was carrying in my heart. It felt like every day I was clearing and cleaning my thoughts and energy. I was being shown that I needed to remind you to do the same.

As my business grows, and I show up more and more to be in service, the time it takes to work through my energy disturbances gets shorter and shorter. Because the truth is, nothing is always going to be perfect, and someone will always say something. I may not be able to control what other people are doing, but I can control how I let it affect me.

Get to know yourself, and give away the stuff that isn't serving you. You are a grain of sand in an energetic ocean. There are much bigger things out there that can carry the weight of worry or fear for you. Let it go. And yes, you can sing that if it helps.

Conclusion

My hope for you is that you realize that being a businesswoman and a mom on your own terms is completely possible. That staying in the pre-fabricated model of what society tells us is suitable for parents is not for everyone. You have permission to create a brand-new model. One that is for you. So riding a unicorn while hanging out with fairies and listening to New Kids on the Block is totally on the table.

The world is so much bigger than what they tell us, and our ability to make a difference far greater. Letting go of the stories that no longer work to create your own is freaking awesome! It's like taking life by the horns and riding it into the sunset.

Choosing to live in your stardust, may seem scary, but it can be the most beautiful place in the land. A utopia of awesome. Waking up every day to serve the people who light you up, anchored in your mission. This is the bomb. This is what I want for you.

Know that resistance and fear also show up every day. Love them fiercely. Snuggle up on the couch with them and watch a movie in your pjs with ice cream. When they are present, chances are you are on the right path. Feeling comfortable and choosing to stay safe is exactly that. Safe. Deciding to boldly stand for what you believe in, what makes you uncomfortable to do? That is living.

Today, declare to the Universe you are ready to shine. That you want to release your old thoughts to bring in the new world. One you can't see clearly but are excited to make friends with.

Stars are meant to shine. And you, my friend, are a star.

Acknowledgments

There are so many amazing people who helped to make this book possible. Firstly, I would like to thank my family. My husband and kids have been super patient in allowing me to become the most amazing version of myself this year. Two books, and three programs later. It's time for us all to play.

I want to thank all the amazing people at The Author Incubator, who helped me find my wings so I could fly. Angela Lauria, Maggie McReynolds, Mila Nedeljkov, Paul Brycock, thank you from the bottom of my heart.

For everyone who joined The Chakra Business Academy and opened to shifting their lives in magical ways for this book. Thank you. Every chapter is filled with the amazing people who trusted me with their journey and I am so grateful.

I also want to thank you, the reader. Your magic is a gift that I love and honour. Thank you so much for energetically connecting with me through this book. To celebrate everything about you, I've created a seven-day energetic blueprint series. This will allow you can connect even more with the energy in your chakras. Hop over to **www.magicalbusinessmethod.com/energyblueprint** to open up your chakras even more.

Life is a gift, that is why it is called the present. Thank you to everyone who makes every day brighter than the last.

About the Author

Tamara has gone from broke single mom to retiring her now husband in only five short years. In early 2017, she downloaded that she could read chakras, and from that point on she committed her life to helping other moms step into the light that they were born to shine. Her mission is to change the perception of what parenting looks like and to create a world where things can be easy and abundance is for everyone.

Tamara lives in St. Catharines, Canada with her husband, Jeff. She has four incredible children, two cats, and two dogs. She loves everything cheesy, like boybands and romantic comedies. Her secret obsession right now is YA fantasy box subscriptions.

Thank You

I love each and every one of you who opened this book and committed to reading it from the introduction to the conclusion. You rock!

As a thank you, I've created a video series based on the chakras that will give you loads of detail about your current energetic blueprint. Each morning for seven days, you will receive a chakra video by email. Sign up at **www.magical-businessmethod.com/energyblueprint**.

I will be drinking a tea in each video so grab yourself your favourite beverage, and let's spend a few minutes in the morning together!

"In two years we've created over 250 bestselling books in a row, 90% from first-time authors." We do this by selecting the highest quality and highest potential applicants for our future programs.

Our program doesn't just teach you how to write a book—our team of coaches, developmental editors, copy editors, art directors, and marketing experts incubate you from book idea to published best-seller, ensuring that the book you create can actually make a difference in the world. Then we give you the training you need to use your book to make the difference you want to make in the world, or to create a business out of serving your readers. If you have life-or world-changing ideas or services, a servant's heart, and the willingness to do what it REALLY takes to make a difference in the world with your book, go to http://theauthorincubator.com/apply/ to complete an application for the program today.

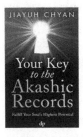

Your Key to the Akashic Records: Fulfill Your Soul's Highest Potential

by Jiayuh Chyan

...But I'm Not Racist!: Tools for Well-Meaning Whites

by Kathy Obear

Who the Fuck Am I To Be a Coach: A Warrior's Guide to Building a Wildly Successful Coaching Business From the Inside Out

by Megan Jo Wilson

A Graceful Goodvye: A New Outlook on Death

by Susan B. Mercer

Lasting Love At Last: The Gay Guide To Attracting the Relationship of Your Dreams

by Amari Ice

Finding Time to Lead: Seven Practices to Unleash Outrageous Potential

by Leslie Peters